CreditRepair

Using the Secret of Section 609
of the Fair Credit Reporting Act

ANDREIA B. McQUEEN-FEAGIN

RENWICK PAUL FEAGIN

DISCLAIMER

This book is designed to provide information and motivation to our readers. It is sold with the understanding that the publisher is not engaged to render any type of psychological, legal, or any other kind of professional advice. The content of each article is the sole expression and opinion of its author, and not necessarily that of the publisher. No warranties or guarantees are expressed or implied by the publisher's choice to include any of the content in this volume. Neither the publisher nor the individual author shall be liable for any physical, psychological, emotional, financial, or commercial damages, including, but not limited to, special, incidental, consequential, or other damages. Our views and rights are the same: *You are responsible for your own choices, actions, and results.*

For permission requests, write to the authors:

ANDREIA B. MCQUEEN-FEAGIN
RENWICK PAUL FEAGIN
P.O Box 2755
Niagara Falls, New York 14301

Printed in the United States of America

TABLE OF CONTENTS:

Our Story

Greetings:

CREDIT IS KING! Having good credit truly has its rewards and advantages. Imagine these yourself:

- ☑ Visiting the auto dealer and hearing the word... ***APPROVED!***

- ☑ Shopping for a loan at a Bank... again...***APPROVED!***

- ☑ Shopping for a home mortgage... ***APPROVED!***

APPROVED is the word you'll always want to hear. No one wants to ever be turned down for what they want and deserve (ex: the finer things in life).

Years ago, Andreia and I, struggled with bad credit. Frustrated about getting turned down over and over, we decided to do something about it.

Unfortunately for us what some creditors reported or didn't fully report to the big 3 nationwide consumer reporting agencies: *Equifax, Experian,* and *Trans Union* were NOT a true account of what happened.

What appeared on our credit reports were countless errors and electronic false information which they voluntarily supplied to them digitally.

There were no physically signed original documents or contracts that could verify anything about what had taken place. It was just their word

As a result of their misinforming inaccurate reporting of our information, it caused us to NOT gain credit with other potential valued credit providers over the years.

Our credit reports were inaccurate but were supposed to be a true reflection of our spending habits and our overall financial transactions that were reported to the big 3 Credit Reporting Agencies.

Instead of allowing our situation to continue, we decided to fight for what is deservingly ours. We deserved better and we developed a plan to go for our goal.

Like you, despite not being an attorney nor certified public accounts we searched for help, and through trial and error we finally figured out what works which resulted in the development of this book.

As a result of our success, we have compiled this book with an easy-to-do 4 Phase Method to aid you to make sure the work you put in to repair your credit will be permanent and not just a temporary fix.

Our do-it-yourself 609 Credit Repair solution self-help book delivers above and beyond details that supply you with a complete layout of descriptive steps you need to follow to fight back against inaccurate information that appears on your credit report.

WHY THE SECTION 609 SOLUTION?

Because 609 is the secret legal law loophole created for the protection of consumers by way of Section 609 of the Fair Credit Reporting Act (FCRA); a legal leeway that helps you to see what's on your credit report to ensure that it is correct.

If there exists anything that has been reported incorrectly to credit reporting agencies it grants you the power to dispute that item and have that certain negative, inaccurate information from your credit reports be removed.

This act details the right of a consumer to receive the following by request in writing:

☑ Contents of your consumer credit files.
☑ The creators of that information
☑ A list of every employer that has inquired about your credit report within the past two years (except for completing an investigation).
☑ All soft inquiries (when a lender or credit card company checks your background of credit to preapprove you for an offer) within the past year.
☑ A full description of their dispute process

[Read more about the Fair Credit Reporting Act in its entirety at this link: https://www.consumer.ftc.gov/articles/pdf-0111-fair-credit-reporting-act.pdf]

So, read each chapter fully and follow our recommendations. It worked for us and we believe it can help you to gain the APPROVED lifestyle you desire too.

What's Your Purpose?

As with all things before going into what seems like a difficult mission you must have a clear motive to be successful.

No matter what it looks like going into any battle a true soldier will tell you:

...it's not about the battle but the fighting spirit that is within you.

No matter how bleak a situation may appear when it comes to your financial situation as the saying goes there is always light at the end of a tunnel.

Well...THIS BOOK IS THAT LIGHT when it comes to increasing your credit score.

Whether your purpose is to buy a house, a car, get-out-of-debt, or simply gain control of your financial status you have bought the right book.

Our goal is to inform, inspire, and enable you to get what you desire.

What we have put in this book will work for you when you are dedicated, determined, and have a true fighting spirit.

Like a candidate running for an office, we must treat this mission as a political campaign with a focused platform.

A political platform is based on what you stand for (ex: FREE Medical Coverage for all) in this case you stand for great credit.

Your platform is what you will stick with until you have met your goal.

Your platform will enable you to win your fight.

Your platform will involve your unwavering ambition to see this goal happen despite being challenged in what will be a letter-writing debate.

WHY LETTER WRITING?

Writing a letter, notarizing, and sending it by certified mail is the best way to build a legal paper trail that will benefit you beyond a telephone call or an online dispute processing website if their negative actions ever cause you to seek litigation.

SO, WE SUGGEST THAT YOU NEVER DISPUTE AN INACCURATE ACCOUNT ONLINE NOR BY WAY OF A TELEPHONE CALL.

As verbal negotiations can be forgotten OVER TIME and processing a dispute online can prolong you're getting the results you need on time, you will want to develop a legal paper trail that can equip you with all you need in a court proceeding if it ever has to result to that.

So, again keep in mind your purpose of why you are fighting... which is again, for that APPROVED lifestyle you desire—which you can have when you don't ever give up or give in.

•   •   •   •   •

On the next page is a sample of affirmations that confirm your platform that you will want to adopt to boost your credit score.

We suggest that you repeat the following statements until you feel it deep in your gut:

#1. I [say your name] … deserve excellent credit

#2. I [say your name] … will do what is required to gain excellent credit.

#3. I [say your name] … will commit to working towards getting any misinformation or unverified information on my credit report removed and or deleted.

#4 I [say your name] … will not let up until the task is completed.

#5 I [say your name] … will handle this matter professionally and respectfully; and will keep the faith until the battle is won.

Now that's said, clap it up, give yourself a hand, and claim victory over this situation.

Now in the duration of this credit repair campaign if for any reason you begin to lose faith get back to repeating those affirmations.

When said wholeheartedly they will supply you with the drive to help you finish your mission.

Furthermore, before we officially begin we would like to prepare you mentally for the battle journey.

Listed below are a few very important topics and the page they are located that we will cover first.

Now let's understand the...

Facts About Your Credit History

☑ Your debt is owned by the original creditor, not the credit bureaus

☑ Information about your credit history is electronically reported voluntarily to the nationwide Big 3 consumer credit reporting agencies who receive no paperwork from your furnishers of credit

The furnishers of credit are the very people who pay them to post it on your credit history report

☑ Reporting your information to the bureaus is not mandatory. Your furnishers of credit can choose whether to report to them or not. IT'S THEIR CHOICE

☑ Your credit history begins when you receive a line of credit from a credit lender (bank, credit union, store, etc.) in the form of a bank card/store card, bank loan, automobile or house purchase, and they track your borrowing, spending and on time or late payment habits

☑ Keep in mind that 85% of your FICO score is based on (your habits) how you manage your accounts and 15% is based on (your history) how long you've had credit.

☑ Below is the full breakdown of what makes 100% of your FICO Score:

The factors that are used to determine your FICO Score

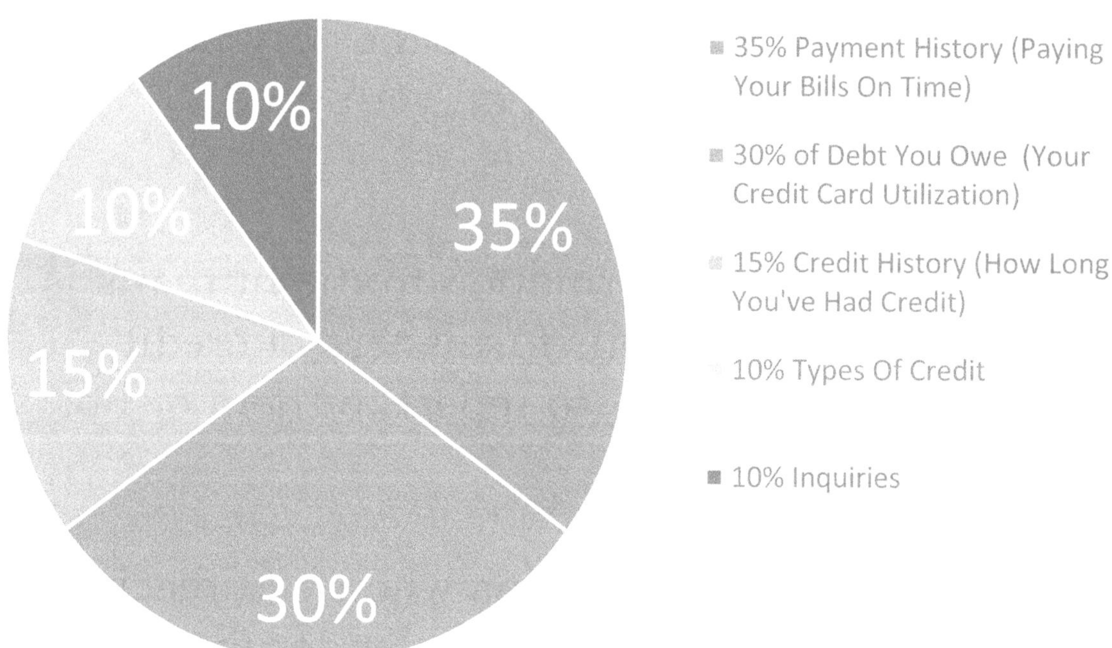

☑ FICO Credit Score Range from 300 to 850:

800-850:	Excellent
740-799:	Very Good
670-739:	Good
580-669:	Fair
300-579:	Poor

- High FICO scores have their benefits and privileges which allow those who have them to receive numerous options of savings and access to what is considered the APPROVED *'finer things in life'* now (if that is what they desire) and pay for them later

- Low FICO scores cause lenders to believe that you are high risk and can result in your paying additionally (with interest)

☑ Not all credit bureaus receive the same electronic information at the same time; it depends on who and when a creditor chose to report it to; each credit agency collects data independently

- o Some companies that provide credit (including smaller banks and debt collection agencies) do not report to all three credit bureaus

- o Public record information as bankruptcies, tax liens, garnishments, etc., is sometimes gathered by each credit bureau by sending a person down to the courthouses to thumb through the records

- o There may show variations among your credit reports from the BIG 3 credit reporting agencies due to different people, reporting the same public record information differently or at different times.

- ☑ Everything that is on a report MUST BE:

  - Within the allowable reporting period (which is typically 7 years for accounts and 10 years for judgments and bankruptcies)
  - Verifiable - All data furnishers must have documentary proof that there is a legal collectible debt

- 100% Accurate - all items and parts of the items that are reported on a credit report must be ACCURATE. It is unacceptable and against the law for part of the item to be reported inaccurately.

☑ Besides lenders there are others who concern themselves with your credit reports and credit scores:

- Insurance companies count on credit scores to help determine your rates

- Landlords check your credit report when deciding if they'll rent their apartment to you and how large of a security deposit to demand you pay

- Utility and Rent-to-own companies screen your credit to decide if they will allow you to open an account or lend equipment to you o That job you've applied for may use the information found in your credit reports to decide if you're a good candidate to hire

o Your credit report can even be used to verify your identity, and for other purposes defined by federal law

☑ It will cost you nothing but a first-class stamp, an addressed letter, and an envelope to get you started (see page 21)

☑ For more information about Credit History and Credit Score check out these reliable resource links:

https://www.experian.com/blogs/ask-experian/credit-education/improving-credit/improve-credit-score/

https://www.creditkarma.com/advice/i/quick-tips-build-credit

https://www.americanexpress.com/en-us/credit-cards/credit-intel/ways-to-build-credit/

Let's Get Ready to Rumble!

First things first, you will need to send for your FREE annual credit report.

The Fair Credit Reporting Act (FCRA) requires each of the nationwide credit reporting companies — Equifax, Experian, and TransUnion — to provide you with a free copy of your credit report (from all three credit bureaus at the same time), at your written request, once every 12 months, if you ask for it.

This one letter will provide you a credit report from all three agencies.

You can accomplish this by customizing a letter in an envelope with a First-Class Stamp to the following address:

Annual Credit Report Request Service

P.O. Box 105281

Atlanta, Georgia 30348-5281

On the next page is a template to help you get started.

YOUR FULL NAME
STREET ADDRESS, CITY, STATE, ZIP CODE
SOCIAL SECURITY#: 000-00-0000 | **DATE OF BIRTH:** 00/00/0000

Date: ____/_____/______

Annual Credit Report Request Service
P.O. Box 105281
Atlanta, Georgia 30348-5281

Dear Sir or Madam:

I [*your name*] ... am writing in regard to request my free annual credit report from all three credit bureaus. I have attached my proof of identification and social security card as well to verify my identity.

Sincerely,

____

Your Full Name

Enclosures: *Copy of My ID Card/ Driver's License*

Copy of my Social Security Card

ATTACHED IS A COPY OF MY

ID CARD/ DRIVER'S LICENSE

YOUR ID CARD/ DRIVER'S LICENSE

...AND MY SOCIAL SECURITY CARD

YOUR SOCIAL SECURITY CARD

Great Job!
You Did It!

The Credit Report Arrives, What's Next?

Now that you have received your Credit Report, first breathe, TAKE A DEEP BREATH IN and BLOW THE AIR OUT SLOWLY.

The good news is that the law is on your side (details on page 28). **Now follow the steps below.**

Step 1: **Review your credit report fully.**

Step 2: **Look for the following errors and check the box(s) that best represent what you see on your credit report.**

Step 3: **Be sure to write the credit account number below the issue it describes.**

☐ Wrongly reported accounts belonging to other people with the same or similar name as yours appear on:

Acct#_______________________________

Acct#_______________________________

Acct#_______________________________

Acct#_______________________________

☐ Errors in your identity data, such
as wrong name, phone number, or
address appear on:

Acct#___________________________

Acct#___________________________

Acct#___________________________

Acct#___________________________

Acct#___________________________

☐ Incorrect accounts resulting from
identity theft appear on:

Acct#___________________________

Acct#___________________________

Acct#___________________________

Acct#___________________________

Acct#___________________________

☐ Wrongly reported account status such a closed account is still reported as open appear on:

Acct#_________________________________

Acct#_________________________________

Acct#_________________________________

Acct#_________________________________

Acct#_________________________________

☐ You're wrongly reported as the owner of the account, even though you are just an authorized user appear on:

Acct#_________________________________

Acct#_________________________________

Acct#_________________________________

Acct#_________________________________

Acct#_________________________________

☐ Accounts wrongly reported as late
or delinquent appear on:

Acct#_________________________________

Acct#_________________________________

Acct#_________________________________

Acct#_________________________________

Acct#_________________________________

☐ Incorrect date of last payment,
date opened, or date of first
delinquency appears on:

Acct#_________________________________

Acct#_________________________________

Acct#_________________________________

Acct#_________________________________

Acct#_________________________________

☐ Same debt listed more than once
appear on:

Acct#_______________________________

Acct#_______________________________

Acct#_______________________________

Acct#_______________________________

Acct#_______________________________

☐ Balance account errors with
incorrect current balance or an
incorrect credit limit appear on:

Acct#_______________________________

Acct#_______________________________

Acct#_______________________________

Acct#_______________________________

Acct#_______________________________

☐ Accounts with data mismanaged
that appear multiple times with
different creditors listed appear
on:

Acct#_________________________________

Acct#_________________________________

Acct#_________________________________

Acct#_________________________________

Acct#_________________________________

☐ Incorrect information reentered on
your credit report even after it was
corrected appear on:

Acct#_________________________________

Acct#_________________________________

Acct#_________________________________

Acct#_________________________________

Acct#_________________________________

**Now that you now know
what you are up against
study the rules on the next page
so you can win.**

#1. Go into this dispute with the fair understanding that the law favors you—you are innocent until they provide full verifiable documented evidence of proof that they indeed are accurate—YOU ARE SIMPLY CHALLENGING THEIR ACCURACY. Their failure to provide that documented proof disqualifies them to by law to collect on it.

- This means that according to The Fair Debt Collections Practices ACT (FDCPA) it is required by debt collectors who are not the original creditors to provide proper debt validation. They must grant you the right to receive the following valid documents of proof that it is a debt that you owe:

- A copy of the original contract with the name and address of the original creditor with your signature on it verifying that you owe the debt
- Everything that is listed on the report is within the reporting period which of 7 years for accounts and 10 years for judgments and bankruptcies
- Every part of each item reported that is listed on your credit report is 100% accurate. It is unacceptable (and against the law) for any part of the credit report to be reported inaccurately and must be corrected immediately and or deleted

#2.   You are going to develop a paper trail of communication with the credit reporting agencies by letter. We

recommend you use the letter
templates we mention in the 4 phase
section on page 42 of this book to write
and get notarized before signing
sending each one through certified mail
only with "return receipt requested," to
each of the big 3 consumer credit
reporting agencies.** By doing it this way
a representative from their company has
to officially sign to receive it which gives
you legal proof that it was sent to their
office. You should be sure you have each
copy you send photocopied and saved for
your own records as well.

#3. **Only dispute an error with the credit
bureau that displays it on their record.**

  - *For instance, if it appears on Trans
    Union credit report only—then only
    dispute it on Trans Union and not
    Experian nor Equifax if it doesn't
    appear there too.*

#4. **Once you dispute an item (by certified
mail) each credit agency you dispute**

has 30 days to investigate and respond to your claim in writing (this does not include mail time and delivery). If an item results in a change or deletion, the credit reporting company cannot put the disputed information back in your file unless the information provider verifies that its accurate and complete.

#5   **If you choose to personalize your own disputing letter we suggest that you keep in mind...YOU ARE CHALLENGING THEIR ACCURACY.**

So, no long sad dramatic stories. And do not admit fault or express guilt. Using words such as:

- *I messed up*
- *It got too much for me*
- *I made a mistake*
- *I became overwhelmed*

...or using foul language (or slang) should not be included. They can result in your being ignored, unsuccessful and legally they could use your very words against your defense and cement your debt.

Instead, use clear understandable language and present yourself as a respectable, professional who is calm, rational, and confident, one who can and will fulfill your demands of verifying or deleting the inaccurate accounts that appear on your credit report.

#6   Disputing challenges may arise causing your results to vary as each person's situation is unique.

This means it may take one or all four phases to accomplish the goal of getting your inaccurate accounts verified or deleted.

However, with persistence and patience, you will get a win over and over each time if you stay in the fight and don't ever give up.

After all, your future plans depend on a good FICO credit score and this is exactly the way to achieve it. Doing so will allow you to elevate your score to gain the lifestyle that you desire and deserve.

Now that you have done the following:

- ☑ ***Received your credit report which lists all information from the Big 3 credit agencies about your credit history***

- ☑ ***Listed the issues that are on your credit report***

- ☑ ***Examined the Ground Rules of Disputing***

…it's now time to use the contact addresses of the big three nationwide consumer credit reporting companies: ***Equifax, Experian, and Trans Union*** use each of the addresses below in your written dispute letters:

- ☐ **Equifax**
  P.O Box 740256
  Atlanta, Georgia 30374

- ☐ **Experian**
  P.O. Box 2002
  Allen, Texas 75013

- ☐ **Trans Union**
  P.O. Box #2000
  Chester, Pennsylvania 19022

Let's Get Right To It!

Get in the ring and start disputing

THE FOLLOWING PAGES CONTAIN 4 PHASES FOR YOUR WRITTEN DISPUTE LETTERS

- *Be sure to customize each letter to cater to your situation and use them wisely.*

- *Complete them in order and give each a reasonable time to work.*

Phase 1

PHASE	YOUR ACTION
1	• Send your notarized and signed **Phase 1 - Written Letter of Dispute** separately to all bureaus by way of certified mail with "return receipt requested," whose report list the issue(s) that has yet to be verified. This letter will serve as their first warning shot; recalling federal law and what needs to be done. • Wait for a written response. • If they remove all issues from all three of your Credit reports, you are done. Great Job! • However, if no response or response results with their saying: *"it has been verified"* be sure to move to **Phase 2** if they have not acted nor removed all the unverified accounts from your credit report.

YOUR FULL NAME
STREET ADDRESS, CITY, STATE, ZIP CODE
SOCIAL SECURITY#: 000-00-0000 | **DATE OF BIRTH:** 00/00/0000

Date: ___/____/_____

Credit Reporting Agency
P.O. Box Address
City, State, Zip Code

Dear Sir or Madam:

You are reporting inaccurate information and I am making a formal dispute. Credit reporting laws require you to report information that is TRUE and MUST BE VERIFIED or DELETED (Section 616 and 617) of the Fair Credit Reporting Act (FCRA).

I am alarmed that information on my credit report is not accurate and I am requesting that it be investigated within the 30 days that the Federal Law requires. Listed are inquiries that I request to be verified or deleted.

Please verify or remove immediately the following:		
Account (Listed by number)	Account#	Status
Creditor 1: KMART CREDIT CARD	Ex: 0000000000	Unverified

*Please remove anything that is over 30-days of non-account holding inquiries and also please add a Promotional Suppression to my credit file.

Thank You,

____

[YOUR NAME HERE]

IN WITNESS WHEREOF, the said party has signed and sealed these presents the day and year first above written.

Signed, sealed, and delivered in the presence of:

____

Signature

STATE OF *[YOUR STATE]*, COUNTY OF *[YOUR COUNTY]*

I HEREBY CERTIFY that on this day before me, an officer duly qualified to take acknowledgments personally appeared

[YOUR NAME], who has produced

______________________________________ as identification and who executed the foregoing instrument and he/ she acknowledged before me that he/ she executed the same.

WITNESS my hand and official seal in the county [YOUR COUNTY] and State [YOUR STATE] aforesaid this ____ day of ____________________ 2021.

____

Notary Public

PRINTED NAME:_________________________________

My commission expires:

ATTACHED IS A COPY OF MY

ID CARD/ DRIVER'S LICENSE

YOUR ID CARD/ DRIVER'S LICENSE

...AND MY SOCIAL SECURITY CARD

YOUR SOCIAL SECURITY CARD

Here's to you!

PHASE 2

PHASE	ACTION
2	<ul><li>Then you will need to send your notarized and signed **Phase 2 - Written Letter of Dispute** separately to all bureaus by way of certified mail whose report still lists the issue(s) that has yet to be verified. This letter will remind them of the first letter and is a legal second warning demanding that they do take some action to resolve the dilemma.</li><li>Wait for a written response.</li><li>If they remove all issues from your Credit reports. You are done. Great Job!</li><li>If no response or response results with them saying *"it has been verified,"* DON'T FRET. *Be* sure to move to **PHASE 3** if they have not acted nor removed all the unverified accounts from your credit report.</li></ul>

YOUR FULL NAME
STREET ADDRESS, CITY, STATE, ZIP CODE
SOCIAL SECURITY#: 000-00-0000 | **DATE OF BIRTH:** 00/00/0000

Date: ____/_____/______

Credit Reporting Agency
P.O. Box Address
City, State, Zip Code

Dear Sir or Madam:

As stated before in my first written dispute letter, under the Fair Credit Reporting Act, Section 609 (a) (1) (A), your credit reporting agency is required by federal law to authenticate by way of physical verification of the original signed consumer contract of any and all accounts you post on a credit report.

Not doing so could result in anyone who pays for your report services the ability to commit fraud to a consumer's account by way of mail, fax, or email.

Please be aware that this is my second written dispute letter concerning the unverified items that I have listed below (once again) that remain on my credit report in violation of Federal Law.

As per your recent investigation you stated in writing that you "verified" that these items are being reported correctly---if so, who verified these accounts?

Under the FCRA you are required to have a copy of the original creditor's documentation on file to verify that this information is accurately mine.

You have NOT provided me a copy of ANY original documentation required under Section 609 (a)(1)(a) & Section 611(a)(1)(A) which should include a consumer contract with my signature on it and Section 611 (5)(A) of the FCRA - you are required to **"promptly DELETE all information which cannot be verified."**

Please act according to the law as there is no confusion about what the written law states that are at hand for me to follow.

If you fail to comply you could be held "negligent noncompliance" according to Section 617. I am willing to take this matter to the full extent of the law to enforce my rights under the FCRA, but I'd rather get this issue done and over with peacefully.

UNDER THE FCRA, I DEMAND THAT THE FOLLOWING UNVERIFIED ACCOUNTS MUST BE REMOVED OR VERIFIED:

Please verify or remove immediately the following:		
Account (Listed by number)	Account#	Status
Creditor 1: KMART CREDIT CARD	*Ex: 0000000000*	*Unverified*

*

Please remove all non-account holding inquiries over 30 days old, and add a Promotional Suppression to my credit file.

Thank You,

IN WITNESS WHEREOF, the said party has signed and sealed these presents the day and year first above written.

Signed, sealed, and delivered in the presence of:

[PRINT YOUR NAME HERE]

____
Signature

STATE OF [YOUR STATE], COUNTY OF [YOUR COUNTY]

I HEREBY CERTIFY that on this day before me, an officer duly qualified to take acknowledgments, personally appeared [YOUR NAME], who has produced ____ as identification and who executed the foregoing instrument and he/ she acknowledged before me that he/ she executed the same.

WITNESS my hand and official seal in the county [YOUR COUNTY] and State [YOUR STATE] aforesaid this ____ day of ____________________ 2021.

____
Notary Public

PRINTED NAME:_______________________________________

My commission expires:

ATTACHED IS A COPY OF MY

ID CARD/ DRIVER'S LICENSE

...AND MY SOCIAL SECURITY CARD

Phase 2
Is Complete!
Hats off to you!

PHASE 3

PHASE	ACTION
3	<ul><li>Then follow with your notarized then signed **Phase 3 - Written Letter of Dispute** to all bureaus by way of certified mail whose report (again) still lists the account issue(s) that need to be verified.</li><li>Wait for a written response.</li><li>If they remove all issues from your Credit reports. You are done. Great Job!</li><li>If no response or response results with their saying *"it has been verified"* be sure to move to **PHASE 4** if they have not acted nor removed all the unverified accounts from your credit report.</li></ul>

YOUR FULL NAME
STREET ADDRESS, CITY, STATE, ZIP CODE
SOCIAL SECURITY#: 000-00-0000 | **DATE OF BIRTH:** 00/00/0000

Date: ___/___/___

Credit Reporting Agency
P.O. Box Address
City, State, Zip Code

Dear Sir or Madam:

Under the Fair Credit Reporting Act, Section 609 (a) (1) (A), your credit reporting agency is required by federal law to give proof by way of physical verification of the original signed consumer contract of any and all accounts you post on a credit report. Not doing so could result in anyone who pays for your report services the ability to commit fraud to a consumer's account by way of mail, fax, or email.

I [YOUR NAME]... hereby demand to see Verifiable Proof from you which includes **an original Consumer Contract with my Signature in it** that you have on file of the accounts I have listed for you below. Your failure to positively verify these accounts has hurt my ability to obtain credit. **PLEASE BE AWARE THAT THIS IS MY THIRD ATTEMPT TO RESOLVE THIS MATTER PEACEFULLY.**

UNDER THE FCRA, UNVERIFIED ACCOUNTS MUST BE REMOVED and if in case you are unable to provide me a copy of the verifiable proof, I request that you remove the following accounts I have listed below immediately.

Please verify or remove immediately the following:		
Account (Listed by number)	Account#	Status
Creditor 1: KMART CREDIT CARD	*Ex: 0000000000*	*Unverified*

*Please remove all non-account holding inquiries over 30 days old and add a Promotional Suppression to my credit file.

Thank You,

[YOUR SIGNATURE NAME APPEARS HERE
AFTER IT HAS FIRST BEEN NOTARIZED]

IN WITNESS WHEREOF, the said party has signed and sealed these presents the day and year first above written.

Signed, sealed, and delivered in the presence of:

[PRINT YOUR NAME HERE]

____
Signature

STATE OF [YOUR STATE], COUNTY OF [YOUR COUNTY]

I HEREBY CERTIFY that on this day before me, an officer duly qualified to take acknowledgments personally appeared

[YOUR NAME], who has produced

____ as identification and who executed the foregoing instrument and he/ she acknowledged before me that he/ she executed the same.

WITNESS my hand and official seal in the county [YOUR COUNTY] and State [YOUR STATE] aforesaid this ____ day of ____________________ 2021.

____
Notary Public

PRINTED NAME:____

My commission expires:

ATTACHED IS A COPY OF MY

ID CARD/ DRIVER'S LICENSE

YOUR ID CARD/ DRIVER'S LICENSE

...AND MY SOCIAL SECURITY CARD

YOUR SOCIAL SECURITY CARD

Phase 3

Is Finished!

You're awesome!

PHASE 4

PHASE	ACTION

| | • And if you still have not gotten all the adverse accounts off your credit score you will need to send your notarized then signed **Phase 4 - Written Letter of Dispute** (again) separately to all bureaus by way of certified mail whose report list the issue(s) that need to be verified.

• Keep in mind by now mostly all unverified accounts should be removed by now. If this has not resulted in your favor as of yet. Save all their responses (which will serve as legal proof for you in the event you have to legally use them in court.

• Again, keep in mind the Fair Credit Reporting Act, Section 609 (a) (1) (A) law favors you. You will be equipped with everything you need if a court case needs to happen. |

YOUR FULL NAME
STREET ADDRESS, CITY, STATE, ZIP CODE
SOCIAL SECURITY#: 000-00-0000 | DATE OF BIRTH: 00/00/0000

Date: ____/ ____/ ______

Credit Reporting Agency
P.O. Box Address
City, State, Zip Code

YOU ARE HEREBY NOTIFIED OF PENDING LITIGATION IN PURSUIT OF RELIEF AND MONETARY DAMAGES UNDER FAIR CREDIT REPORTING ACT SECTION 616 AND SECTION 617

The purpose of this final written letter is to OFFER A SETTLEMENT BEFORE LITIGATION as my effort to resolve your continued violation of the FCRA by way of your refusal to delete UNVERIFIED information from my consumer file.

Include the following words if they provide you with a written response that says that it has been "verified" without them giving any proof with your signature on it:

As per your recent investigation you stated in writing that you "verified" that these items are being reported correctly---if so, who verified these accounts? You have NOT provided a copy of <u>ANY</u> original agreement contract (an agreement with my signature on it) as required under FCRA Section 609 (a)(1)(A) & Section 611 (a)(1)(A).

65

PLEASE HEED MY WARNING as it is my intent to prevent an occurrence of litigation under the **FAIR CREDIT REPORTING ACT to seek relief and recover all monetary damages that I may be entitled to under Section 616 and Section 617** if you continue to refuse to delete unverified items I have listed to you in three previous written attempts. Your failure to do so will be used as a part of my formal complaint to the Federal Trade Commission.

Every notarized written copy (which I photocopied too) I have sent you will serve as documented proof of your failure to comply with the **FAIR CREDIT REPORTING ACT along with this additional offer of settlement.** Correct this matter and comply with the law.

Again, I demand the following accounts below be verified or deleted:		
Account (Listed by number)	Account#	Status
Creditor 1: KMART CREDIT CARD	*Ex: 0000000000*	*Unverified*

*Please remove all non-account holding inquiries over 30 days old and add a Promotional Suppression to my credit file.

Thank You,

IN WITNESS WHEREOF, the said party has signed and sealed these presents the day and year first above written.

Signed, sealed, and delivered in the presence of:

[PRINT YOUR NAME HERE]

____
Signature

STATE OF [YOUR STATE], COUNTY OF [YOUR COUNTY]

I HEREBY CERTIFY that on this day before me, an officer duly qualified to take acknowledgments, personally appeared [YOUR NAME], who has produced

_______________________________________ as identification and who executed the foregoing instrument and he/ she acknowledged before me that he/ she executed the same.

WITNESS my hand and official seal in the county [YOUR COUNTY] and

State [YOUR STATE] aforesaid this ____ day of _______________ 2021.

____
Notary Public

PRINTED NAME:_______________________________________

My commission expires:

ATTACHED IS A COPY OF MY

ID CARD/ DRIVER'S LICENSE

YOUR ID CARD/ DRIVER'S LICENSE

...AND MY SOCIAL SECURITY CARD

YOUR SOCIAL SECURITY CARD

Phase 4

WELCOME TO THE FINISH LINE!

Take a bow!

You did it.

A Few Last Words...

Now with your credit disputes behind you and you've gained the knowledge to continue to defend yourself in the future with an increased credit score, we recommend that you continue to stay informed of your credit score with the use of credit helping apps—such as Credit Karma, Credit.com, myFICO or others.

We also recommend that you get a copy of our book **What's My Financial Info** (check out our offer on page 70) to keep you organized.

By now we are sure you have found success in your quest to gain the APPROVED LIFESTYLE you desire. Now you can buy that car, boat, and house; increased your credit score, and developed that peace of mind knowing that all is well in your financial world.

Whether you completed all 4 phases to reach your desired goal to correct or remove all unverified information from your credit report or ended the battle early and there are no more battles to dispute then we say...

"WELL DONE!"

However, for those of you who will have to continue with litigation, we want to remind you that if you have followed all steps to achieve progress to remove or delete unverified items off your credit report you have put your best foot forward.

You have done the work yourself and developed a paper trail of communication that favors your benefit in a court of law.

To begin filing a lawsuit and sue the bureaus you will need to first file a complaint at the following Federal Trade Commission, which is the government organization that protects your rights as a citizen of the United States of America.

You can do this by reporting on their website at this web address below:

https://reportfraud.ftc.gov

Be sure you follow through with every step that the website gives and complete anything they recommend that you complete in a timely manner.

It has been reported many times in the past that others have had to result in litigation and won. Here are a few website links that can give you more about that information:

- [ ] https://www.ajc.com/news/state--regional/credit-errors-upend-lives-thousands-consumers/UrgLhTkNsv8VNbWEFpZi7O/

- [ ] https://www.prnewswire.com/news-releases/transunion-sued-in-federal-class-action-for-continuing-to-misreport-innocent-consumers-as-terrorists-on-credit-reports-despite-previous-punitive-damages-verdicts-against-it-for-similar-misreporting-301118210.html

We wish you the best of luck with all that you strive to do. Thank you for your patronage.

- The Feagins

Check Out This Offer!

Get our #1 book that has room for you to write down all of your important WEBSITES, URLs, USERNAMES, PASSWORDS, & PURPOSE for your banking, school, online shopping, social media, utilities, and more... so you won't ever have to worry about forgetting them.

Pick Up Your Copy Today Online!
Now available at

https://bit.ly/Whatsmypassword